C000054747

Enjoy the Book

Life is for Living

© Inte / Phoenix Rising High 2015
This edition is published by Phoenix Rising High, Amsterdam, The Netherlands
Authors Inte & Chiara Alfonso
Design & typography Lisa Scheer
Illustrations Elske Berndes, Emanuel Eschner, Cebine Nieuwenhuize,
Marielle Schuurman, Marc Weikamp
Font https://www.yanone.de/
ISBN 978-90-824254-0-6

be a
better
you

As I drove my daughter Chiara to one of her friend's house we began to talk about all manner of things — philosophical discussions, jovial matters, and what life is all about. Towards the end of the conversation my daughter looked at me and said "Dad, you really have to write a book about these things". I laughed it off, dropped her off and wished her a good day. Three days later I was sitting on a plane flying to Amsterdam and I struck up a conversation with the person sitting next to me, and for 45 minutes we talked at length about almost everything under the sun, then to my surprise I heard "you know, you should write a book". Four days later, I was sitting at a cafe drinking coffee and a complete stranger came up and asked if he could sit with me as all the tables were taken, I said "sure, pull up a seat", we talked for almost two hours, and then I heard him say "well, I think you should write a book". I reflected on this, within one week I heard the same message 3 times, and without further ado I made the decision. I went back to my daughter Chiara and said that I would write the book if she wrote it with me, and thankfully she agreed.

The book is written as a set of short stories that are concise and to the point and coupled with an illustration to help further the message. Each illustrator was given a set of stories and asked to draw freehand what he/she interpreted and to visualise it into an illustration. The illustration is also a unique view of the story by the illustrator and bonds the intended message for the reader. The simple messages and stories are a written invitation to you to awaken yourself and interpret as you wish and formulate your own thinking, passion, and desire to make your life better each and every day.

LOVE YOURSELF

Often we forget what love really is. We often say we love our mother and father, our friends, our pet cat, but what does it mean when we say we love someone or something.

Love is a word that we use over and over again to relay emotion(s) that we feel, however in reality it is a word we don't truly understand. Love is an emotion that comes from deep within ourselves.

Therefore the most important thing about love is that you have to love yourself. Why is it important to love yourself, because once you love yourself you know what love is and then you know how to love others.

What does it mean to love yourself? You're born into this world, you've been given a vessel which is your body, a mind which allows you to use your body, and a world in which you can project your mind, body and spirit into. Learn to love and accept all these things and use them to their fullest extent.

Love is the most fundamental emotion you have which when projected outward is the most powerful asset you have in your life. This flow of energy (or love) will shape the world around you.

To love yourself, you have to learn to be happy with yourself and let the inner energy within yourself shine and radiate out.

MAKE TIME

In our busy life we do the things we have to, and let the things we want to do pass us by. Time will pass by and nothing of what we want will be accomplished, just the yearning of the 'what ifs'. This should not be the case.

We have to make time also to do the things we want to do in our life.

Make a concerted effort to make your life an enriching life by actually making time to do the things you want. If you wish to learn the guitar, buy a guitar and set aside time every day or every week to learn to play the guitar. If you wish to paint, make time to get the canvas and paints and then let loose your creativity on the canvas.

Wanting to do things is one thing, but making the time to do them is the reality that you need, so throw away the shackles of believing that you have no time to do anything and make time available to yourself to do what you want.

Time is something that we can never gain back; so use it to your utmost in your life.

Relationships are one of the most rewarding aspects of life's adventures; they provide you with friendship, love, happiness, fun, and excitement. When in a relationship we hold the other person so tight in every way, wanting that person to be our everything – we do this from a position of love.

Sometimes, we disagree with the person we are in this relationship with. We become passionate about whatever we are in disagreement about to the point that we have only one aim, and that is to win the argument at hand (whatever it may be, and in the most part it is something which is mostly inconsequential and in the big scheme of our lives has very little impact).

Winning the argument becomes our main focus, not whether we are right or wrong, but because we want to prove our point, make sure the other person sees that we are right and they are wrong. By winning the argument we prove that we are right. How wrong can you be!!!!!

The argument causes undue stress for both of you, it causes a small rift in your relationship, it shows a somewhat ugly nature deep within you, it infuses your relationship with a little anger and doubt, and above all 99% of the time it is a meaningless argument. Maybe the argument was not needed in the first place.

Understand what the argument is about, realise that winning is not the goal, but rather that the argument has dissipated and become something of a benign conversation that results in nothing more than both of you laughing at each other at how silly it was to start in the first place and find something better to do with the time that could have been wasted arguing.

HASTE MAKES WASTE

When embarking upon a task don't rush, take your time, and be diligent and as accurate as you can be as the task at hand should be a reflection of the perfection that you are trying to attain.

Pay attention to the details, and make sure that you have done your research and have given 100% of yourself.

The completion of the task and the result of it is a reflection of both your ability and knowledge and thus to rush it would be doing an injustice to yourself.

When you take time to do something you also have to make sure that you give all of yourself to the task and in this way you will derive great satisfaction of the end result and also will have learned more than you would have if you had rushed.

At college or school we tend to do our assignments because we have to, why not turn it around and think of it as an opportunity to also learn and show what we can achieve not only to ourselves but to others.

At work we often do tasks because they need to be done, but why not go a step further and also learn how to do it better or differently with a better outcome.

Be the best you can be in whatever you do.

The desire for conflict in humanity is very strong, and often there is always some sort of conflict between friends, lovers, family, and even at your work place.

Conflict in the majority of times that you encounter it, is a very negative situation and that can lead to your valuable time, energy, and emotion being drained with worry and the unknown and how to handle the situation. So there is only one remedy for this.

Remove conflict from your life, make a stance.

Change conflict to a challenge that you need to overcome, rather than something that is standing in your way. Take the conflict, turn it around to something that you can solve right away. In this regard you seek a solution rather than envelope yourself in the worry about the conflict.

One example for myself was in a work situation where one colleague of mine was always creating chaotic issues and being in conflict on a personal level with many of the team. His desire to being in conflict was that he wished to win what he perceived was a fight of sorts. Upon seeing this behaviour I decided to act, and the next time we had a meeting I told him that I was not going to fight with him and if he wished to cause conflict in our working arrangement then of course he could, but I would not fight him and let him win. At this remark he was stunned and did not know how to react, needless to say for the coming months and years I never encountered an issue with him.

Basically, I neutralised the potential situation that I could foresee happening thereby removing the conflict that could have been.

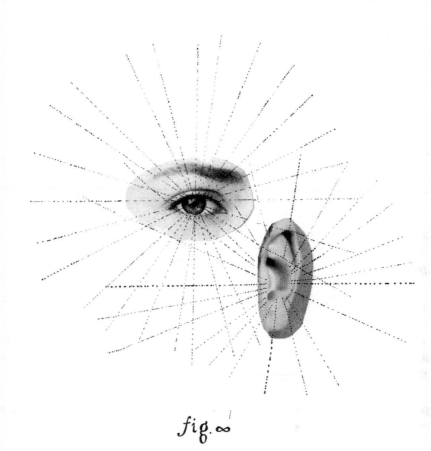

fig. ∞

SELF IMAGE

At any age it is hard to feel content with yourself for who you truly are and all the flaws that go with being you, as a teenager this can be even more challenging.

Let's face it nobody is perfect. Perfect just doesn't exist and who you are on the outside doesn't define you. Everyone is different and everyone has attributes of themselves that they like and some that they dislike, but it is important to not envy another; be happy in the person you are. Love yourself and be your own person because everyone is beautiful in his or her own way. Having confidence in yourself and the way you look will increase happiness and give you a much healthier life style.

Present yourself in the best way possible; you cannot change the way you look, but what you can do is be the best version of yourself. Have high self-esteem so that you are not restricted from doing the things you want to do, because you lack confidence in yourself. As the saying goes "Low self-esteem is like driving through life with your handbreak on."

Don't let the opinions that others have on you define who you are. Rely on the opinions you have about yourself and aspire to be the person you want to be, not the person others want you to be. Walk with your head held high and many doors will open for you.

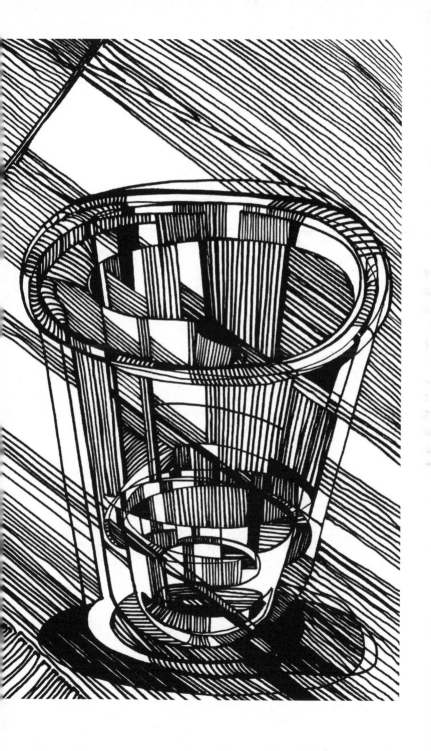

When you look back on the life you have lived so far, think of all the positive things that you have achieved, the good things that you have done, and if you feel that you have missed out on something there is still time to make sure you can do what you want to.

Reflect, choose a quiet place where you can close out the world for an hour or so and let your mind be free and wander aimlessly until you stumble upon something that sparks your interest and then use this reflection to create the opportunity to explore the new avenues in your life.

It is by reflecting that we sit still and view our life and realise what else we wish to do.

Our lives have become more and more busy. Communication is faster, people's expectation of hearing back from us is that it should be sooner rather than later, and it seems that we have no time to do anything. Indeed we tend to scramble to get things done because a lot of our time is already taken up it would seem.

Stop.
Pause for a moment, and understand the following:
You are in control of the time you have in your life.

Really, it may not seem so, but you are actually in charge of what you do in your life and when. We all have certain commitments that we have to adhere to, for example being at work at 9am or being at school at 8am – but aside from these we have full control of what we do with the rest of the time we have.

We waste a lot of our time looking for things that we put somewhere in the house, or even frantically looking for something in the morning when we are in a rush to get out of the house. We are wasting both time and energy in these situations.

Learn to use your time wisely. Be prepared for the day to come.

The night before, sit down and ask yourself what do you need for the next day. If you are going to work, have you ironed your shirt, which dress will you wear, what shoes will you wear, is your gym bag ready for your gym class after work... Make sure that you prepare for the day to come.

In the morning, you can relax, have breakfast knowing full well you are ready for the day and will see what adventures you can have. Preparedness allows us to use our time wisely.

TWENTY MINUTES

So, you really, really want to have an argument with a loved one.

Nothing in the world will stop you from having this argument and you have to get it out of your system — Ok, fine.

Have your argument.

Be as nice as you can about it.

Say what you need to say, and again be as nice as you can about it.

One thing — ONLY allow the argument to have a duration time of 20 minutes maximum.

Stop yourself after this 20 minutes.

20 minutes should be plenty of time to allow your feelings, emotions, thoughts, rants, gestures and waving of your arms to communicate whatever it is you wish.

Stop.   Be Quiet.

Reflect.

Understand that you have poured out your heart and soul, and now it is time to get on with life.

Don't waste any more time, you have had your 20 minutes.

TOMORROW IS ANOTHER DAY

The day can be long, full of challenges, and almost never ending. Sometimes it seems that nothing goes your way, and every new task brings new situations that need some resolution.

People around you demand more and more of your time. The tasks at hand seem to be taking longer than you anticipated.

You feel overwhelmed with all the things that need to be done, and time is something that is not on your side.

Wait. Breathe. Think.

Take a look at the tasks you have to complete, list them out, find out what can be done today, and see what is remaining. Notify whomever that the remaining tasks will be done tomorrow as you do not have the time to finish all the tasks you currently have on your list, and show them the list of tasks so that it is apparent to all that you have a lot to do already.

Finish your tasks for today.

When completing your tasks you need to be able to focus and put your whole energy into completing each and every task to the best of your ability, and this should be your modus operandi. You should be always performing at your best, and producing the highest quality of workmanship that you are able as this is the real measure of you as a person.

Tomorrow is another day to turn it all around.

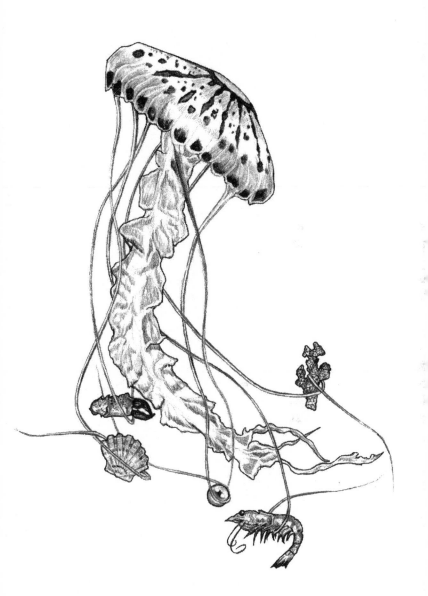

As you grow up you tend to go through the motions of life, school, work, marriage, maybe having children. A small house, a car and some comforts to make your life better.

You should consider what is the purpose of your life.

Your goals, targets, dreams, and what you wish to achieve are different aspects, so what is your purpose in life?

Is your purpose to live a better life than your parents? Is it to serve humanity in some way? Is it to become a teacher to help all those around you better themselves? Is it to make yourself rich?

So consider that as you are born into this world, you need to also establish the purpose of your life.

Having a purpose also allows you to find out who you really are and what you can contribute and this will further enrich your life.

The purpose of a flower is to show its beauty, allows bees to harvest its nectar to make honey, take in carbon dioxide and produce oxygen for the world around.

Have purpose and become a better person.

CHOICES

When faced with a multitude of choices we need to make a choice of one of them to do. Often the choice we make leads to the desired result, however sometimes this choice leads to a result that is not what we wished for or wanted.

When the outcome of the choice we made is undesirable we understand we should have made a different choice. Often we feel aggrieved at the choice made and look back at the decision made and beat ourselves up for making the wrong choice.

We then, having made the wrong choice, more often than not carry on along the path of the choice and end up in an even more disastrous situation. We reflect on how we are perceived on the choice made, and this makes us feel even worse.

One has to realise that in life many choices that we make may not have the desired result, we need to take stock of what needs to happen going forward, and it is in this that one is able to salvage the situation and turn it all around. Learn from the bad choice, and make a better choice next time.

The measure of a person is not by the choices he/she has made, but by how he/she deals with the consequences of the choice when it does not have the desired result.

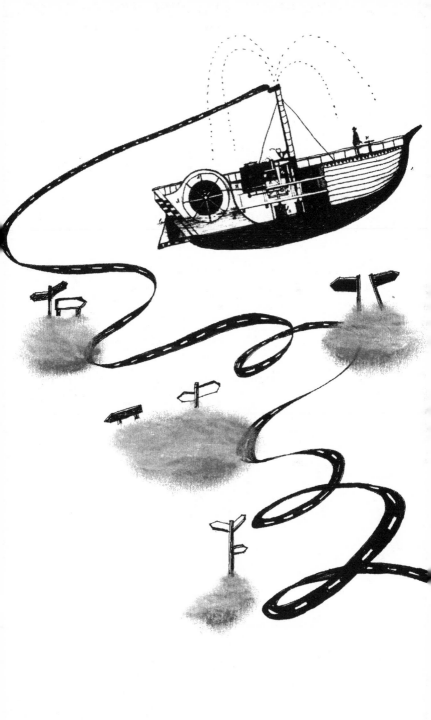

When we were young children we understood very little of how life is, other than some real basic elements of life itself, these being eat, sleep, play, learn.

As we grow older, we keep the 'eat' and the 'sleep', and to a large extent as we go to school we also keep the 'learn'.

What we drop from our childhood is the 'play'.
Why?

So I say onto you, let's get the PLAY back into your life.

Every day should be a **Happy Day**
Every day should contain some **Fun**
Every day should contain some **Adventure**

As humans we deserve to have fun, happiness and adventure in our daily lives; this has helped us evolve into the beings that we are, and let it continue to be part of our whole life and not just the start of our life (as we were children).

Every day our inner child should radiate a little, allowing us to realise how life is one big adventure and being happy and having fun is all part and parcel of living.

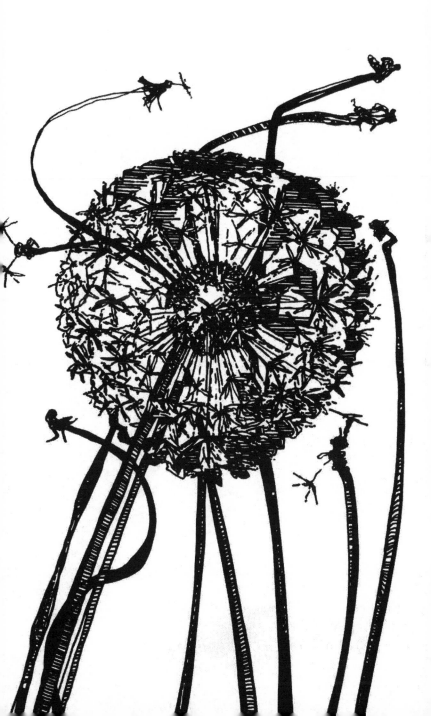

LIVE WITHOUT REGRET

How often have you thought about the past and looked back at certain events and regretted them or even regret not doing them. Today, make a stance; decide that you will live from now on without regret.

Use your moral compass to judge quickly for yourself if the things you wish to do will leave you with anything but a good feeling. When you decide that regret will play no part then go ahead and do what you decided to embark upon without fear.

Freeing yourself from the shackles of regret will broaden your horizons and free your mind. Commit yourself and give it your best shot.

If the result is not what you expected, then understand that you did it to the best of your abilities and try again if you think you can do it better next time around, leave regret out of the equation, as it will only play a negative role in your endeavours.

The positiveness that you will create when you remove regret from your daily life will only enhance your life in everything you wish to accomplish moving forward.

LOVE THE PERSON

When we first meet a person, we view them like an open book. We try and learn what makes them laugh, smile, and what excites them and what they love to do. We are keen to see what we can share with them, see what we have in common and more importantly how they can be part of our life and how together you can both have fun.

You are an individual just as the other person is an individual, you like different things sometimes, you have a different sense of humour, you have different outlooks on life itself. Each person has the ability to help another to learn from themselves and show all the good qualities of themselves, so that together you can have a friendship or a relationship with each other.

The most important aspect of any relationship should be that you accept the person for who they are, and love them for what they are and not what you want them to be. Then, and only then, can you grow together and learn from each other and develop that relationship to a higher level, as equals, as partners or even as soul mates.

The free spirit that you see in the other person should also be reflected in yourself.

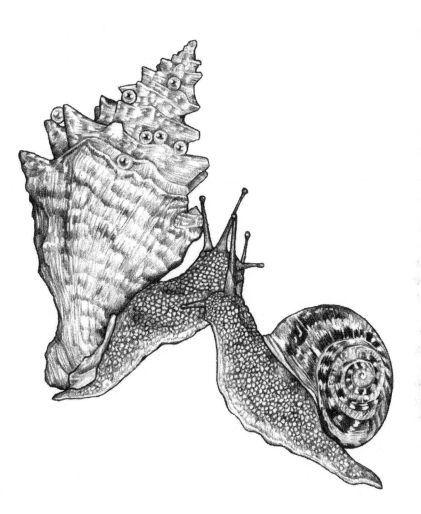

COMMITMENT

When you commit to doing something, make sure you finish what you have started.

This sense of achievement of completion will lead you to start and finish other tasks.

Commitment comes from the desire deep within to achieve and is more than just a word; it is an act or action.

Commit yourself wholly to the task and finish it to the best of your ability.

YOUR GOALS IN LIFE

Life is a beautiful adventure, which we often forget about as we get caught up in the daily events and the endless need to 'survive'; we forget that we also have a choice of what we can do in life.

What do you want to achieve in your life?

Decide on at least 5 things that you wish to achieve, make them small goals so that you can achieve them but not too easy that it takes no effort.

Now, make a plan to make these goals achievable. Start with the first goal, the easiest one that you can (in your mind) achieve.

Focus on the steps to achieve this first goal, and once achieved move on to the second goal.

What you have done is 2 things, (1) you have listed goals to achieve in your life and (2) you have taken the necessary steps to make that goal(s) happen.

You have been able to complete the first goal and realise that you can work towards something you wish to achieve in your life. Now you are ready to start on your second goal, then third goal, and so on.

By achieving the first two goals you have paved the way on how you can set a goal and achieve it, or as I say make it happen. With this you are able to set goals for yourself and know how to go about making your goals a reality.

BE EFFECTIVE

The night before or when we wake up in the morning we often have a number of tasks or items that need to be accomplished — more often than not we let them linger on our mind as the day unfolds and by the evening we realise that we have forgotten to act upon any of the tasks we wanted to accomplish. Why?

We get carried away with the events of the day, and put off doing the things we need to do until we have finished what is at hand, however as the evening approaches we have not even started any of the tasks we needed to have done — these can be anything as small as writing to an old friend who sent us a email or letter, paying the electricity bill, or even at your job reviewing the analysis that a colleague has sent you to get your reaction.

To be truly effective, one should make a list of tasks to get done for that day, and then pick the least favourite task on the list and get that done first, then pick the next least favourite task and finish that up. What remains will be a small list of tasks that will be a joy to do, and your mind will be free and fully focused on accomplishing all tasks on your daily list.

Effectiveness comes from doing the things that we are required to do or things that are necessary to finish, and then the rest of the day feels like a weight has been lifted off your shoulders.

As you make a list for each day and complete the tasks you listed, you begin to realise that you are truly being more effective in your life and achieving more day by day, and this will help you towards your long-term goals.

MAKING IT LOOK EASY

In my first 'big' job after I graduated I was lucky to be doing something I really loved and enjoyed, and with this I put all my energy and effort to performing to the best of my abilities and producing the desired result that was needed. My boss at the time was one of the most supportive people I had ever met up until that point, and he took me aside one day and said the following: "The work you are doing is amazing and I see all the effort and time you are putting into it, but you make it look so easy, can't you at least make it look hard and complicated so that others in the team see how incredibly motivated you are and what you are accomplishing. You look like a swan floating gracefully across the lake, but I also want you to show the team that under the water you are paddling your legs furiously!!"

I was taken aback by his comments, which were relayed to myself almost in a paternal manner. I couldn't believe what I was hearing, how could it be that it mattered how it seemed to others so long as I got the job done. I thought about his comments all evening long, and came to the realisation that what he wanted me to do was show others in the team of all the sacrifices I was making and all the extra effort I was putting in so that I would lead by example and inspire others around myself to also perform to the best of their abilities.

The next day I was in the office I held a small team meeting, and decided to show everyone in the team about the project I was completing and the difficulties I was having and how I was overcoming them – this led to many positive questions being asked and a total involvement of the team in my small project to work together with me. As a team we grew closer and worked better together, just by communicating clearly with each other.

Always have a plan.

More often than not, the person with a plan has that plan (or some semblance of it) put into action. Why you may ask?

Most people tend to want to debate or discuss or talk about possibilities, 'what if' scenarios and eventual outcomes when trying to think about putting a plan of action together. This kind of discussion is great for brainstorming sessions, but not when it comes time to make decisions and move forward with a plan of action.

In general a person will not formulate a plan unless he/she is asked to, and herein lies the opportunity for the person that wants to 'make it happen', where it being the item being planned. This person has the proactive attitude that the item being discussed will be implemented and therefore if he/she can make a plan for it then that plan will be on the table to be actioned upon.

People don't generally like to stick their neck out, and hence the person with a plan should also make sure that he/she is armed with all the information regarding the project at hand and make sure that all eventual outcomes are shown and with enough detail to make sure that plan is solid when being presented to others.

Often said "He/She who dares, wins".

DON'T LIE

In life we face many situations where we think a small lie that we tell will have no consequences or impact, but quite the opposite is true.

Once you decide to tell a lie, it has to always remain a lie, and you have to store this lie in your memory so that you can make sure you are consistent with the untruth you have told in the time to come. The fact you have to remember this lie for the rest of your life is counterproductive to being able to be an honest person who has nothing to worry about. When other people catch you out in the lie you told, then it places you in a vulnerable position of trying to justify why you told the lie in the first place, and this creates doubt in others as to your character and you as a person.

You tell a lie to cover something up or to embellish something that you wish others to hear; the question is why did you tell this lie. Because you wanted to appear as someone you want others to think you are or because you were scared to tell the truth and decided a lie was the best option.

So, maybe you should decide the following: instead of lying maybe it is best not to say anything or say that you wish not to say anything — and thus the lie is averted and your integrity and character is intact.

My father once told me as a child, "If you tell a lie, you will need to tell a million more lies to cover up the first lie, is this the way you want to live...?"

You are standing in a room, waiting for the instructor to tell you what to do. The instructor and you are on the fifth floor of a building, both of you are facing an open window. The instructor tells you to jump out the window. You walk over to the window and look out of the window and see that there is a large drop all the way to the ground. The instructor asks you again to jump out the window, you hesitate, why should you jump out of the window and fall five floors down.

Stop. Think.

Your mind is racing, how is it possible the instructor wants you to jump out the window and fall five floors down onto the ground. The most probable outcome would be that you will hurt yourself, or may even break a leg. Your heart races, fear takes over.

Stop. Think. Breathe deeply.

Your mind freezes. Your heart races faster and faster. You have to jump, else you have failed the test at hand. You look at the instructor, he tells you to jump.

Stop. Remain calm. Breathe deeply. Think differently.

So you jump onto the window ledge, look at instructor and jump back into the room. You have jumped out the window!!!

When faced with a problem that we don't know how to solve, we immediately revert to what we know and in this case our thought was to jump out of the window falling five floors — however, our one-dimensional thinking would not have saved us as we had to learn how to think differently and know that you could jump out of the window back into the room.

We must learn to think, act, and consider a number of possibilities, not just to do the first thing that comes into our mind or react to the situation.

CONDUCT

One needs to live by a set of morals and principles and apply these to all aspects of one's life. Then and only then is one able to be a complete person and know that they are true to themselves and this is reflected in how others perceive them.

A friend of mine was on a train heading into work, and he heard some commotion as someone was getting on the train, as he lifted his head he saw a young man enter the train apparently swearing and behaving rather belligerently to some fellow passengers with whom some sort of altercation had occurred. As the train pulled out of the station the young man was still grumbling at the fellow passengers until a time when he stopped and pulled out a newspaper and started reading. My friend got into work, and set about his normal day, in the afternoon he was interviewing someone for a position at the company and to his surprise the young man who was on the train causing a commotion entered the room ready to be interviewed for the position being offered. The interview got under way, and the normal questions were asked, and then my friend decided to ask the question of how his day was going, to which the young man replied it was a pretty good day. My friend pressed on by asking how his train journey was today, the young man looked startled but managed to compose himself and answered that it was fine. My friend then realised that this was not the right person to work at the company due to the fact that he had already told an untruth, and proceeded to inform the young man of the situation that he witnessed earlier on the train. The young man had no answer and understood that the position of Customer Relations Manager was not going to be offered to him.

Be true to yourself always and to others, and be nice.

MISTAKES

In life we make choices, some easy, some difficult and some without even thinking about them.

We also make mistakes, mostly based on our choices. We kick ourselves for making these mistakes, but remember this:

It is ok to make mistakes.

It is a way of learning.

However, if you must make mistakes, don't make the same mistake again, make a different one!!!

NAYSAYERS

As you embark on a new adventure in your life, the excitement that you feel and the sense of intrepidation is one of the best feelings that you can experience.

You may wish to share the new adventure with others, and hope to see the excitement in others as you envisage it in yourself. However not everyone has seen the same vision or feels the same way as you do. This is normal.

Others may not share your excitement, but don't let this deter you, they may try to put you off your new adventure, but why? This adventure is something you have created for yourself, something you wish to happen and have fun with, others don't see what is deep within you and what drives you. So, I say to you, don't let the naysayers put you off your new adventure, they don't understand the desire to have this adventure and can't see how it will make a difference to your life and well being.

Listen to the naysayers, reminding yourself that you have the ultimate decision to do what you wish. Tell them of your excitement and that you will embark on the journey and see where it takes you — let the naysayers know of your resolute action in making this adventure happen and be fun — if they want they can be part of it, but in reality it will be you and only you that will embark on this adventure and learn from it and succeed in whatever way you wish.

Be strong and resolute, and enjoy the new adventure.

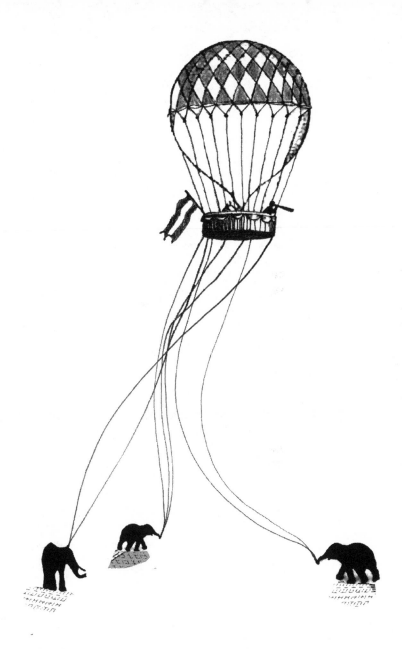

If you can keep your head when all about you
Are losing theirs and blaming it on you;
If you can trust yourself when all men doubt you,
But make allowance for their doubting too:
If you can wait and not be tired by waiting,
Or, being lied about, don't deal in lies,
Or being hated don't give way to hating,
And yet don't look too good, nor talk too wise;

If you can dream — and not make dreams your master;
If you can think — and not make thoughts your aim,
If you can meet with Triumph and Disaster
And treat those two impostors just the same:.
If you can bear to hear the truth you've spoken
Twisted by knaves to make a trap for fools,
Or watch the things you gave your life to, broken,
And stoop and build'em up with worn-out tools;

If you can make one heap of all your winnings
And risk it on one turn of pitch-and-toss,
And lose, and start again at your beginnings,
And never breathe a word about your loss:
If you can force your heart and nerve and sinew
To serve your turn long after they are gone,
And so hold on when there is nothing in you
Except the Will which says to them: "Hold on!"

If you can talk with crowds and keep your virtue,
Or walk with Kings — nor lose the common touch,
If neither foes nor loving friends can hurt you,
If all men count with you, but none too much:
If you can fill the unforgiving minute
With sixty seconds' worth of distance run,
Yours is the Earth and everything that's in it,
And — which is more — you'll be a Man, my son!

RUDYARD KIPLING

PRACTICE MAKES PERFECT

To be better at something one needs to do. However, to be the best one needs to do over and over and over again until almost perfection is achieved.

The idea that doing something once will achieve the perfect result is something that we believe is possible, but 99.99% of the time this is not the reality. One must practice.

The practice of the task at hand, when done many times, allows us to learn from each step of how to do something better and also allows us to learn what we can do differently to achieve the perfection that we wish to attain.

To be an Olympic champion at anything not only comes from talent, desire, and the will to succeed but also from the fact that practicing every day will ensure that.

Practice makes perfect through repetition. Then the task becomes second nature when you perform it since you have performed it many times over.

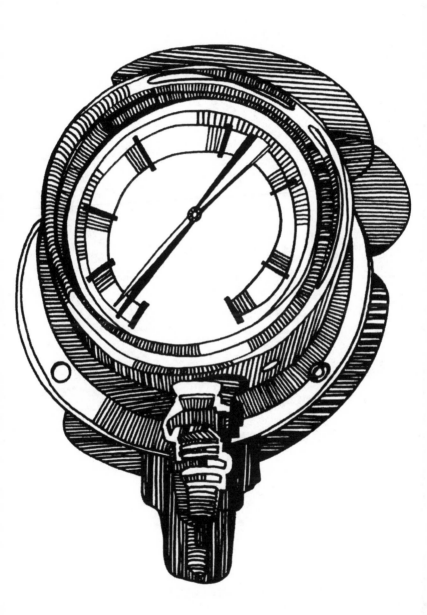

When faced with adversity and situations that require great courage and humility there is a small poem/prayer that can help you deal with whatever is at hand, it is:

> Grant me the serenity,
> To accept the things I cannot change,
> The courage to change the things I can,
> And the wisdom to know the difference.

The essence of this poem is why should we worry about the things that we cannot control, but rather we should do something with the things that we can control and make our lives better. It is far better to spend your time and energy on the things that you can have influence over and change.

The past is one of the things that we are unable to change, however we can and should learn from the past. We have to have the courage to face this reality that we are unable to change the past and see what we can do going forward instead of dwelling on what could have been, one should focus on what can be!!!

SUCCESS

To be successful one must follow a set of guidelines:

Focus on what you can do better

Become a powerful listener

See play as an essential for creativity

Make desire flow into steps you can act upon

Be persistent and persevere

Be disciplined

Remember the devil is in the details

Less rush, more focus

Inspire yourself

INSPOiRe YOUR Self

CHAOS IS YOUR FRIEND

When faced with chaos many people freeze, do not know what to do, and in some cases panic.

Use chaos as an opportunity that allows you to dig deep and make sense of the things that are going on.

Turn chaos into your friend by embracing it and solving the issues that it creates.

Learn that chaos is nothing more than something that is not understood or manageable, and then once you label it you can work on it to understand it and use it as a challenge to solve the chaos at hand.

Break chaos down into small pieces that you can understand and rectify.

Let chaos be no more than a riddle that can be solved.

When we encounter any emotional pain in our lives, we stop and try to make sense of the pain, and sometimes we wallow in the pain — feeling some sort of self-pity or acknowledgement from others that we are in pain.

Why do we want to suffer? Is suffering the key to a happy life? The answer is obvious, no!!!

Emotional pain is something that we need to overcome, learn from and understand, so that we can help ourselves to stop it occurring again. Obstacles in life cause us pain in many forms, however we should choose to use the pain to make us stronger and to become more resilient to the thought of pain being something bad in our life.

Use any pain that comes your way, and turn it around; let the pain pass through you and understand that you have the ability to control how emotional pain affects you.

Emotional pain can inflict weakness in your life, and this weakness should not interfere with the positive forward thinking you have. Weakness is something that can be turned to strength by not allowing it to overcome your feelings or emotions or your mind.

Gain strength from adversity and don't numb pain, use the pain to overcome those things that are hurting you by making yourself mentally stronger and being prepared to know what pain can do to you and that you will not let pain hurt you.

Pain is just another obstacle to overcome in the pursuit of happiness.

Scores of decisions are made almost every day by each of us. Some decisions are made quickly, others need a little time for reflection or investigation, nonetheless decisions are made.

In this fast paced world that we live in now, we are more and more asked to make decisions faster than we used to. The speed of communication necessitates that information is sent and that a response should be forthcoming as soon as possible.

When making a decision, understand the 2 forms of response: action and reaction.

Action: Take all the information you have, look at as many possible outcomes and solutions, evaluate the best options and then decide what action to take.

Reaction: When presented with a situation that offers very little time to think, act swiftly.

Above, I state that in both cases you should ACT, but in one case you should act swiftly — which means you should know you have a certain time period within to act. Always make sure you have thought about the information you have before you arrive at any decision, it should be well thought out.

Never react, always act.

A famous quote says:
"Think like a man of action, act like a man of thought"

MAKE A START

Dreaming of what we want to be, what we want from life, and sometimes where we want to be; these are some of the roads that we travel down in our conscious and subconscious mind. We imagine the highest feats we wish to accomplish, the rewards from the attainment of those feats and the absolute satisfaction and joy that would come our way. And then, reality hits, we have to get ready for school, work, the baby needs changing, the driveway needs clearing of the snow that fell the previous night.

What just happened!!!! We entered a world where we could dream a little, of what could be. So, what is stopping us?

In all of us is a dreamer, and for most of us that is exactly where it stops: in the dream world. We stop at the point where we see in our dream world what feats we want to accomplish and what it feels like to accomplish them and the justly rewards. We see the end goal, however what we don't see is how to start the journey towards that end goal.

If you really want your dream to happen, then you have to make a concerted effort to find out how to start.

The hardest part of any journey, whether it is a dream to fulfill or a task to complete, is to understand that the first steps are the most important and that you have to embark on the start of the journey to be able to make it happen.

Decide if you really want to make your dream a reality, and then make a start on it, then, and only then will you have completed the most difficult stage, i.e. the start.

MUST HAVE, SHOULD HAVE, CAN HAVE...

The fundamentals in one's life is what you must have to survive, what you should have to have a good life and what you can have to further enhance your life.

You must make sure you have a roof over your head for yourself and your loved ones, must have food to eat for all those you are responsible for, must be able to clothe yourself and loved ones adequately. You must take your responsibilities seriously.

You should get an education to better yourself, you should have a purpose in life, you should have dreams and goals and ambition to drive yourself to be a better person. Above all you should do good for yourself and all others around you.

You could have a better home than you have, could have a better car than you have, a better computer than you need, could have a newer wardrobe.

You have to decide what is important for you, and make sure you take care of the must haves and should haves before you entertain any thought of the could haves...

LAUGH

Laughter is the music of the soul, and the more you laugh the more your inner spirit shines and the contagious nature of laughter becomes infectious to those around you.

It is said that you need less muscles to laugh than it does to frown.

The body, mind, and spirit are light when laughter is in the air and this feeling is truly something that will uplift you.

Joy and laughter go hand in hand, and the sensation of enjoying yourself will be reflected in the way you laugh.

A day without laughter is a day that is unfulfilled.

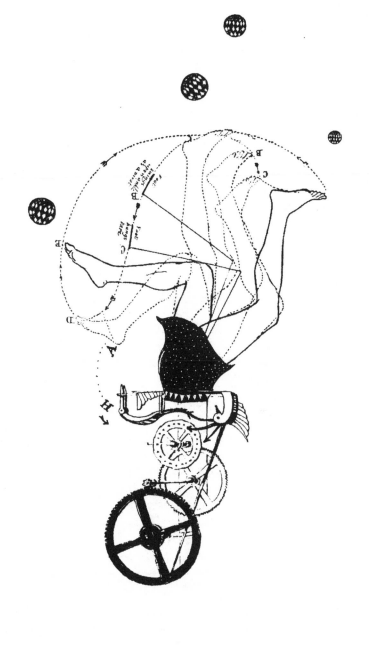

PROCRASTINATION

There is a saying that goes "the road to hell is paved with good intentions", and many a person always has good intentions to do a certain task but never really gets around to it. Why do we do this to ourselves? Why do we say we will do something, then finally at the last moment have to rush to do it or never do it?

We procrastinate, doing the things we wish to do rather than the things we promised to do or need to do.

When we leave tasks to the last minute, we fail to realise that we are actually hindering our ability to be productive, to use our time effectively. Often, the task(s) that we defer in this manner are not of vital importance however as time goes on we 'feel' that we should do them at 'some point' and this is a feeling that lingers until the task is completed or the time to have the task done has elapsed.

We carry this task on our shoulders in an unconscious manner, and it plays on our mind every now and then. Does this help us focus on the things we want to focus on? Unconsciously we become a little anxious about this deferred task.

So that we can be free, and creative and use all the time we have to achieve the best from ourselves, we need to realise that procrastination is something that we should shun from our everyday life. Do what we need to do, and then we are free to focus on all the other life enhancing and fun activities we wish to engage in.

Remove procrastination from your life, and your mind will be free to be creative.

BRIGHT EYED AND BUSHY TAILED

As one awakes in the new day, one should awake refreshed, ready for the day, and the adventures that it can bring.

The new day is the key to another day in your life that will give you some fun, some happiness, and some adventure.

Wash your face, brush your teeth, look back in the mirror at the wide-eyed face staring at you, and know that today is a day to make your life and your world a better place to be in.

Being bright eyed and bushy tailed each and every morning allows you the ability to allow the world around you to help you better yourself each and every day and live a fulfilling life.

Big smile, face the world, and make a difference.

Another day, another adventure...

WHO HAS MORE?

We see what others have and don't have, and also what we have and don't have, so the natural question arises of who has more? The simple answer to this is — does it matter?

What matters is what you have, and what you can achieve with the little you already have to make your life better.

Is it envy, is it part jealousy, or is it partly greed of how to perceive what others have compared to ourselves? The motivation of wanting more should not be driven by negative emotion but rather from the desire to achieve more for yourself to make your life a better life.

At the end, who are you really competing with other than yourself to make your life both meaningful and fulfilling.

MEDIOCRITY

When embarking on doing a task, do we start by making sure the task is done with only the minimum effort possible, and thus ensuring that when the task is completed it is not done with all the effort we can muster?

One should abhor mediocrity in all things, as this is a symptom of a lack of effort, motivation, and drive on your part. One should use all your energy, all your knowledge, and above everything all your passion to complete the task to the fullest of your abilities and capabilities. Only then, can you truly say you gave it all and you will feel a sense of achievement and some sense of pride.

Half-heartedly doing something never bears any real fruit and almost never gives you a sense of having achieved something — since you just wanted to complete the task at hand for the sake of having it completed rather than actually enjoying the act of completing the task and seeing it finished and realising that you put all your effort into it.

When one lives a mediocre life, one must understand that the outcome of that life is anything but ordinary.

Therefore, strive to do the best at whatever task you have at hand, relish the journey along the way, you may learn something new, and have that feeling of accomplishment that you always yearn for.

Shun mediocrity and strive to become the culmination of the best of your abilities.

REMOVE FEAR

Fear is an emotion that comes to us all at some point in our life; the key is how to deal with fear.

Let fear pass through you, overcome it and realise that it is just a mere emotion that had some intrinsic personal value, which when you reflect upon you begin to realise that it is only a manifestation of your lack of confidence and ability leading to a feeling of dread.

Fear is the mind killer.

Fear holds us back from doing the things that we want to do or need to do — the fear of failure or even the fear of success. The intrepidation that fear creates debilitates us from doing what needs to be done.

Remove this fear by understanding that it will never contribute to a positive outcome, and thus you allow your mind to breathe again and see the world around you as a limitless amount of possibilities.

What we expect from others does not entirely occur in reality, as our expectations do not sometimes match the actions of the people we are dealing with. In this regard, we should understand that what we expect does not manifest itself and we should move forward in a positive way.

Is it because we are not clear in what we expect from others, or is it that we did not communicate what we want or wish for? This is a question only you can answer.

However, to allow ourselves to carry on we sometimes have to realise that we will be disappointed and try to figure out why that is the case; and if possible we should identify the root cause and see how to rectify it or make sure it does not happen again. The end result is that we are disappointed, but we should learn not to be disappointed but embrace it to learn from it.

A story relevant to this is that of the frog and the scorpion: A scorpion wishes to cross a small river but is unable to as he is not able to swim across it, and thus upon seeing a frog asks the frog to help him by having the frog carry him on his back. The frog says to the scorpion "but you are a scorpion and you will sting me", to which the scorpion replies "No I won't since if I sting you while you are carrying me on your back across the river we will both drown", to which the frog hesitantly replies "Ok, but promise me you won't sting me and then I will help you" to which the scorpion agrees. So the frog carries the scorpion on his back across the river and as they near the middle of the crossing the river becomes more stronger in its current, and the frog still manages to keep going but the scorpion is afraid and fears for his life, and when the frog becomes unbalanced in the water the scorpion becomes even more afraid and stings the frog, to which the frog replies "You have stung me, and we are both going to die now, why did you do this". The scorpion replies, "I am sorry, but it is my nature".

COURAGE AND ENCOURAGEMENT

We live in the days of reality television and numerous talent shows where people throw themselves unwittingly at the mercy of judges and the general public to see if they are able to showcase what they love to do in the hope that they will win. For all those who do not succeed it can be a bitter disappointment, even though they gave it everything.

These people have the courage to go onto television and show their talents. They dream of winning. This is a fine dream and an example to us all of how we should dream and chase our dreams to make them a reality.

However, the judges are often cruel to the contestants and shatter all their dreams with their insidious remarks. This is the injustice that humanity suffers that a few can decimate the talent of the many and not realise that they have destroyed their dreams and aspirations.

We should encourage those who wish to dream and allow them to make their talents even better — for they are doing what is the best of their ability. We should applaud those contestants for their courage. We should encourage them to better themselves.

Alas, we have been told that only winners can be applauded, and of those there are only a few.

For all those people who have dreams we should encourage them and not belittle them, such should be humanity.

GIVE OF YOURSELF

One should give of themselves without want, for then and only then can one truly be free of any preconceived notions and not be caged.

When one gives of themselves with all their heart and mind, it is truly a gift to others, and if others do not accept this in the spirit that it is given then that is a reflection of others' insecurity and closed mindedness.

When one gives and others ignore or do not recognize it, then this should not matter to the giver, as the giver gave with their heart and mind.

By giving of yourself you also open yourself to a wealth of possibilities since your heart and mind are free of what others may think, and this is the ultimate reward for the giver — peace of mind that they gave without want.

EXPECT THE UNEXPECTED

Our expectations of what should be in certain situations arise from what our previous experiences are, what we have read about, and most importantly what we want the desired outcome to be. Mostly we tend to be disappointed with the outcome as it is not the desired result we want.

With this in mind, expect the unexpected. Be open to all possibilities and learn to grasp that not everything you will do and want is within your immediate control.

Learn how to deal with the unexpected by embracing it, by dissecting it, and seeing how you can move forward with it so that you can make the situation better for yourself.

The fun part of anything is sometimes not knowing what to expect and being pleasantly surprised. Here you have been open and receptive to whatever may happen, and accept the outcome. The freedom of this acceptance also allows you to be more creative and willing to see what happens next.

Expectation by definition is a strong belief that something will happen as you envisage it. By expecting the unexpected you will also have opened up yourself to the possibilities of the unforeseen or something that may surprise you — working with the unexpected can lead to something else, something that you did not even imagine. So revel in the unexpected as this is the crucial stepping stone to dealing with when things don't work out the way you want.

Make unexpected outcomes work in your favour.

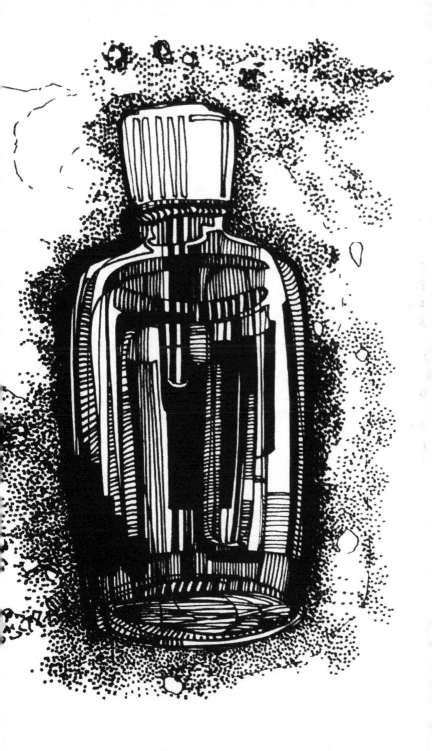

CONTROL

Mastery of oneself is often found within the ability of how we control ourselves. Control of our senses, of our mind, and of our body are often key in many martial arts as the form of mastery. The ability to control oneself is a great gift to have, and one that takes many years to master and is something to be sought and to train so that you can become better at it.

One must always try to attain the highest form of control in oneself, so that one can be free of any constraints in mind, body, and spirit and have a fulfilling life.

However, when one wishes to control another person, then this form of control is an abomination to the human spirit. This form of control says more about you than the other person, it shows that you truly have no control of yourself and merely wish to substitute your own lack of control for a false control over someone else. Whenever you feel the need to control another person understand that it is a debilitating process in any relationship.

The removal of control from any relationship helps cultivate harmony and well being between the people in that relationship, and this in turn results in a free spirit and creative and loving atmosphere that is open to building stronger bonds between those involved.

Master control in oneself, and you will be a free spirit.

LOVE YOUR HEALTH

Our brain controls the functions of our body, it is the greatest instrument that we possess, and use every single moment of our life.

Our body is the greatest vessel that has been given to us at birth and this should be taken care of as it is the only vessel we will ever have.

As you love yourself, learn to love your body, and treat it with the respect it deserves. Look after it, mend it when it breaks and above all know that it has to last you a very long time.

Don't treat your body like a garbage can; nourish it with the right amount of food.

Challenge your body but not to the point of breaking it, endeavour to make it stronger but also remember that moderation is also a valuable measure.

Above all, use your body and mind to their full extent, make sure you take care of your health — once you love your health, your health will give you back generously in all that you do.

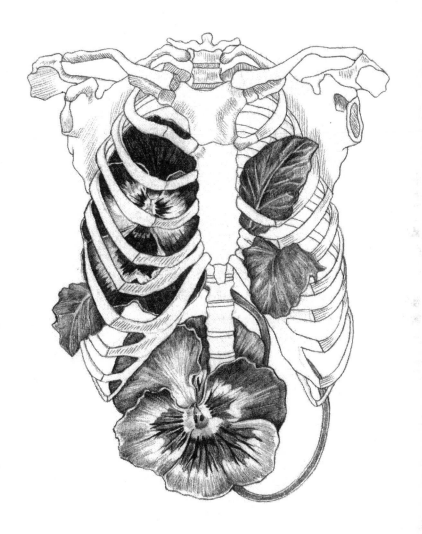

FRIENDS, QUALITY OVER QUANTITY

Throughout your life the people that you surround yourself with and the friendships that you make have a big impact on your life. We all depend on the company of true friends. Friendship brings more happiness than anything else. When we are sad we can turn to a friend and when we are happy we can turn to a friend. A friend should be there for you no matter what.

Sometimes we befriend the wrong people. It is important that your friends don't weigh you down; instead they should be a positive influence on you. Make friends that will better your life and force you to do good things that normally you wouldn't do rather than do bad things that can get you into trouble.

If you can count the number of true friends you have on one hand, you are blessed. Sometimes, especially teenagers can be caught up in popularity and think that the quantity of friends they have makes them more popular. Social media has a big impact on this. Often people obsess over the number of followers they have on Twitter and Instagram or the amount of friends they have on Facebook. However most of these followers and 'friends' are not actually your friends.

Your true friends will be right beside you.

Dream. Dream a realistic dream and aim to achieve it. Don't dream something that is impossible to reach. Have a dream and make it a reality.

Growing up, we have all aimed for the top. Some of us dream to be footballers, pop stars, astronauts, the list goes on. But very few of us go on to achieve these dreams; often as we grow up we start to believe these dreams cannot be reached. If we actually believe that our dreams can come true and work hard for them, eventually we can achieve them. Work hard, dream big.

Dreams can be as little or as big as you want them to be. You can dream to do well in exams, dream to have a healthier life-style, dream to do well in your career. Dreams have no limits; they can be whatever you want them to be, just make sure they are achievable.

Expect obstacles but overcome them; don't let them get in the way of your dreams. Having a dream is just the beginning.

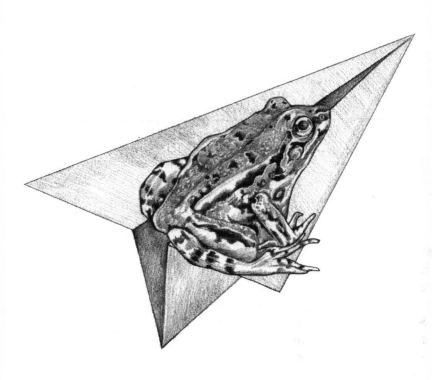

WRITE IT DOWN

We hurry from one place to another, doing something and then turning our attention to something else. Our brain is constantly at work, processing information, making sure the body is ticking over correctly by sending the right signals, and then also it brings thoughts and ideas to the forefront.

Take heed, when your brain is signaling a thought or idea and you stop for a moment to think about it, make sure you do the following: Write It Down.

More importantly, this fleeting thought or idea or inspiration will be active in your brain for about 5 to 10 minutes, unless you make a conscious note to remember it. So, within 10 minutes write it down or even a few words so that you can recall the exact thought or idea. The ability to write it down then enables your brain to continue functioning and focus on other things that come along the way, and maybe you have more interesting thoughts that you need to write down — but this will only happen if you are able to free your mind of the first thought and then your mind is free to engage in other avenues of thought.

In the age of mobile phones, it is possible to make a note of the thought right away.

When you finally read your thought after a time, it will trigger you on an interesting journey of delving deeper or even to branch off to other thoughts.

Never let a thought escape you, write it down — and then act on it.

YOURSELF IN OTHER'S SHOES

Predominantly we are used to being self-absorbed individuals who are so tied up in the fabric of our own lives that we forget how other people see us through their own eyes or how we behave towards others without the slightest notion of what our behaviour actually is.

One must be strong in oneself, however when dealing with others one has to understand or have empathy with the other person. This empathy is more akin to stepping into the shoes of that person and seeing the worldview from their angle.

When you actually see the viewpoint from the other person, you realise and see more than you would ever have seen before, since that person is not you and you have only ever seen from your own viewpoint. This in turn makes you a better person.

Having your own view coupled with the viewpoint of the other person allows you also to make a more informed and holistic judgment of whatever situation you are dealing with.

It is said, "Two heads are better than one".

WEIGHED DOWN

Indulgence is a very human trait that is both good and bad. When you take a look at the animal kingdom you will seldom find any animals who truly indulge to do anything to excess for the sake of it. Wild animals will forage, conserve, and eat what is necessary for their survival and what is needed for the moment; their bodies have adapted to eating and being able to use that food, which is being converted into energy for whatever activities they need to engage in.

As humans we have developed our mental capacity and the science of food technology has enabled us to eat better, live longer, and not have to worry about foraging for food as we used to do or as wild animals do. However, we have taken a step too far in regard to food consumption; we eat when we want to, we eat when we see food that we desire, and we eat when we feel like it, mostly out of boredom. This has led us to being weighed down and our bodies are unable to cope with the sheer amount of food we consume and the feeling of tiredness and laziness reverberates throughout our bodies.

The idea that in this day and age we consume more than we need when food is readily available is a contradiction to the way our internal organs are constructed, and this leads to issues in health in ourselves. So, what can we do about this?

Being weighed down by the over indulgence of food debilitates us and how we function. By eating just enough we are able to respect our bodies and the assimilation of the food and thus have the opportunity to feel good and use the energy derived from the food source in the most optimum way possible, thus giving us the freedom to feel more energetic and being able to do more.

LOVE, HONOUR, AND RESPECT

The simplest principles in life are most often the easiest to wish to live by and the most difficult to maintain, however when you make a resolution that you will live by these principles then over time these principles become the guiding light.

Personally I live by the following three principles that embrace my everyday life and they form the base of my morals.

Love others, as you love yourself and give love to the people nearest to your heart. Love all the things you do.

Be honourable in all your actions, say what you will do and do what you said you would do. Be clear and communicative to all others in your life and avoid any ambiguity. Be honest with your words and your actions.

Respect others, as you would like to be respected yourself. Respect other people's views and thinking. Respect all the tasks you have to do, making sure you give every task the very best of your abilities.

Find a set of principles that you can live by in your everyday life, work hard on them to make sure they become second nature to yourself and then eventually these principles will be embedded in your unconscious mind and will become the essence of you as a person.

Become a better person each and every day.

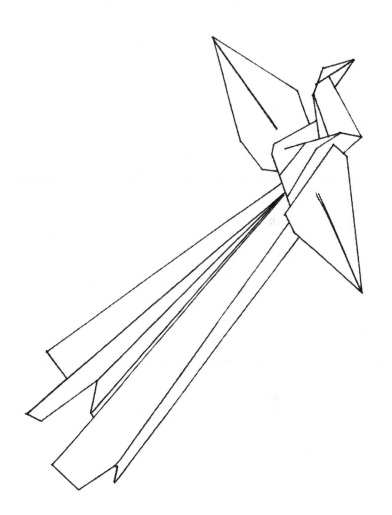

INTE

Inte lives and works both in London and Amsterdam. He commutes frequently between the two locations and runs a business based in Amsterdam. Inte has 4 daughters who live in London. Inte has a strong passion and desire for making the world around him a better place to live in. Creativeness, innovation and determination are his drivers for getting things done. Inte has a "dry and sophisticated" humour that his daughters don't quite understand yet, but they still laugh with him.

CHIARA ALFONSO

Chiara is studying in London, and is the eldest daughter of Inte. Chiara loves to read, write and more than anything socialise with her friends from all walks of life (such is the diversity of London). Chiara loves sport and is currently practicing ju-jitsu. Chiara is an inspiration to her younger sisters (though they would deny that...) and has a rare talent and flair for tripping up on a flat floor.

LISA SCHEER

Lisa is a versatile person. She has a background in English, graphic design, and photography. Lisa has been involved in this project from the start. She searched for the illustrators that would suit the stories and managed the progress of the book. Besides this, she designed the book and made the illustration for the cover.

ELSKE BERNDES made the illustrations for

Think Differently
Make a Start
Happy and Fun
Commitment
Expect the Unexpected

Twenty Minutes
Practice Makes Perfect
Self image
Who has More
Write it Down

https://nl.pinterest.com/elskeberndes/

EMANUEL ESCHNER made the illustrations for

Love Yourself
Chaos is your Friend
Be Effective
Must Have, Should Have, Can Have
Courage and Encouragement

Yourself in Other's Shoes
Haste Makes Waste
Mediocrity
Friends, Quality over Quantity
Don't Lie

http://emanueleschner.tumblr.com/

CEBINE NIEUWENHUIZE made the illustrations for

Love your Health   Give of Yourself
Love the Person   Weighed Down
Courage and Wisdom   Tomorrow is Another Day
Dream it, Do it   Don't be Disappointed
Making it Look Easy   Bright Eyed and Bushy Tailed

http://cebine.nl/

MARIELLE SCHUURMAN made the illustrations for

Make Time   Choices
Reflect and Do   Laugh
Control   Naysayers
Succes   Conduct
Remove Conflict   Overcoming Emotional Pain and Weakness

http://www.marielleschuurman.nl/

MARC WEIKAMP made the illustrations for

Act or React   Preparedness
Remove Fear   The Plan
Procrastination   Mistakes
Live without Regret   Arguing for Time
Your Goals in Life   Purpose in Life

http://www.marcweikamp.nl/illustratief

Made in the USA
Charleston, SC
19 October 2015

the emotional), the lower mental, the higher mental, the celestial (which is also the causal, solar, or eternal body, and what White Eagle later in this chapter calls the Temple), and Spirit.

[10] This passage also occurs in THE LIGHT BRINGER, on p. 105.

[11] Proverbs 29 : 18.

[12] 1 Corinthians 15 : 40.

[13] John 14 : 12: 'The works that I do shall he do also; and greater works than these shall he do'.

[14] The words in inverted commas are a paraphrase of Matthew 7 : 7.

[15] Isaiah 11 : 6. The previous words, about becoming as a little child, are a paraphrase of Mark 10 : 15 or Luke 18 : 17.

[16] Romans 12 : 19.

[17] Philippians 4 : 8.

[18] This and the next paragraph appear in THE PATH OF THE SOUL (W.E.P.T., 1997, pp. 16–17), in two chapters on the Water Initiation, either of which may usefully be read in conjunction with this book.

[19] The three paragraphs which follow are taken from White Eagle's teaching in the book MEDITATION by Grace Cooke (W.E.P.T., 1955, 1999) and are included for their usefulness as a meditation at this point.

[20] The story of the Transfiguration is in Mark, chapter 9, and that of the Pentecost in Acts, chapter 2.

[21] Matthew 7 : 20.

[22] John 15 : 8.

[23] Compare Matthew 6 : 33.

THE WHITE EAGLE PUBLISHING TRUST, which publishes and distributes the White Eagle teaching, is part of the wider work of the White Eagle Lodge, a meeting place or fraternity in which people may find a place for growth and understanding, and a place in which the teachings of White Eagle find practical expression. Here men and women may come to learn the reason for their lives on earth and how to serve and live in harmony with the whole brotherhood of life, visible and invisible, in health and happiness. The White Eagle Publishing Trust website is at www.whiteaglepublishing.org.

Readers wishing to know more of the work of the White Eagle Lodge may write to the General Secretary, The White Eagle Lodge, New Lands, Brewells Lane, Liss, Hampshire, England GU33 7HY (tel. 01730 893300) or can call at The White Eagle Lodge, 9 St Mary Abbots Place, Kensington, London W8 6LS (tel. 020-7603 7914). In the Americas please write to The Church of the White Eagle Lodge, P. O. Box 930, Montgomery, Texas 77356 (tel. 936-597 5757), and in Australasia to The White Eagle Lodge (Australasia), P. O. Box 225, Maleny, Queensland 4552, Australia (tel. 07 5494 4169).

You can also visit our websites at
www.whiteagle.org (*worldwide*);
www.whiteaglelodge.org (*Americas*);
www.whiteeaglelodge.org.au (*Australasia*),
www.whiteagle.ca (*Canada*)

and you can email us at the addresses
enquiries@whiteagle.org (*worldwide*);
sjrc@whiteaglelodge.org (*Americas*); and
enquiries@whiteeaglelodge.org.au (*Australasia*).